THE
FLOWERING
STONE

BOY IN THE WIND

BY

George Dillon

POEMS · 1927

THE
FLOWERING
STONE

BY GEORGE DILLON

New York
THE VIKING PRESS
1932

Some of these poems have been printed in
THE DIAL, THE NEW REPUBLIC, POETRY,
and THE SATURDAY REVIEW OF LITERATURE

PUBLISHED SEPTEMBER, 1931
SECOND PRINTING MAY, 1932
THIRD PRINTING MAY, 1932
FOURTH PRINTING OCTOBER, 1932

To
HARRIET MONROE

CONTENTS

ONE:

TWO:

ANATOMY OF DEATH

THREE:

FOUR:

ADDRESS TO THE DOOMED

ONE

THE NOISE OF LEAVES

ALIVE IN space against his will,
A man may find along his way
Some loveliness to live for still:

He falls upon the earth in May
And hides his face from the cold moon
Whose beauty mocks him when he grieves,
And hears the birds subside, and soon
Only the noise of blowing leaves,

And wonders why his heart grows light
To hear the soft contagion spread
From tree to tree across the night.
He knows that even the jointless dead
Are not so lonely where they sprawl,
Yet knows that he is not alone—

He clings to something after all,
Stretched on a flying flowering stone.

FABRIC OF LIGHT

Now IN the alien crystal of his eye
He turns the wilderness of night to beauty—
Takes from the summer passing without pity
One moment, though the months have wantoned by

Swift as the breeze that slides against his body:
He sees a willow hanging over a stream,
And in the torn moon-whitened grass, a beam
Far flung as from a fiercer moon, his lady.

So charmed asleep and changeless she will lie,
And brought to earth, but only by her lover,
Who stills in flight the glittering flocks above her
Of the starry sky.

SHE SLEEPS

INCIPIENTLY, the hush of death
Lies on her limbs like early snow.
Love, in this light-drawn tide of breath,
Cares little whether it wake or no.

As summer sleeps in autumn's arms,
So every cry and every kiss
And all love's laughter and alarms
Were but a clamouring toward this;

So even the fruit forsakes the vine;
So even the heart's high branch blows bare;
So even her lips are lost from mine
Like leaves upon the flying air.

THE HOURS OF THE DAY

THE CITY stirred about me softly and distant.
Its iron voice flew upward into the air.
All day I wondered that I walked and listened
As if in freedom there—

And wondered how love so led me and removed me:
My breath coming deep and glad, for she had drawn it;
My eyes being wild with pride because she loved me;
My heart being shielded with her beauty upon it.

THE WAKENING

IN THE white mist of morning I took my way
When air and earth were one,
Naked, bewildered, ankle deep in dew,
And heard the trees sigh round, beholding none,
Save where, the dawn being shot with silver day,
The lovely ghost looked through
Of a red flowering maple, that might be
Coral in the sea.

And I sought you,
Saying your name, and where in the world are you hiding?
Out on the meadow? In the miry sedge
Searching for orchises? Or riding, riding
Under the aspens at the river's edge?

But the mist blew about me; it was sliding
Windily over my head before I knew,
And I saw branches blowing and shaken,
And I shook too,
And followed after it, afraid to waken
Into the coloured world whence you are gone,
And reached for it, and wandered where it flew
Full of the rattle of pigeons on and on—
And climbed, and ran, and stumbled, and went still
Up the transpiring terraces of a hill,
In the cold dew of a forgotten dawn.

THE MAD HUNTER

THOSE WINGS still beating all about
Are but loud ghosts of beauty flown;
Yet my desire keeps cocked to shoot.
What matter the vivid game be gone?

I have a hunger food is gall to.
I starve more sweetly on the thought
Of that light thing I could but call to,
That careless image hardly caught.

What matter the snowflakes hush the wood?
What matter the solid rifle rust?
What matter the dark come down for good?
Love goes believing, for it must.

THE CHARM

THE IMPOUNDED spirit pulsing to be free,
I swore by the late moon I would disown
The charm that saves me from the ruinous sea,

And so put out in an old boat alone,
And from its bottom bailed the silver sky,
Then let it sink, and swam myself to sleep,
And wakened heaving when the sun was high
Against the rose-veined adamantine steep
Of a far island wilderness—and lay
And dripped on a black rock where harebells nod
In cracks the spongy moss has overgrown,
And thought I must have died, and thought it odd
My heart beat still on the indifferent stone,

And laughed, and wept, and laughed, and heard all day
The angry gulls shriek over me like God.

THIS DREAM IS STRANGE

THIS DREAM is strange that has not flown
Though summer from the sky has strewn
Her lovely laces on the dust:
This honeysuckle-scent not lost
With all the rain has washed away;
This verdure not exchanged for hay
And bundled up and borne to stall;
This bough most profitless of all,
But freighted with the pain of spring
Unfruitfully—the only thing
In forest, flower-bed, or field,
That still must bloom and may not yield.
Alas! far happier the bare
And dreamless orchard hung with air,
The meadow of its beauty mown,
The garden by the wind brought down
Whereon the sorrowful years depart—
And happier the broken heart,
Whose grieving is a wind gone by.
This love is strange that does not die.

THE SUMMERY NIGHT BEFORE
THE FROST

THE SUMMERY night before the frost
My heart divined the frost was toward.
I saw the lake's wide iris lost
And the red flag of sunset lowered.

I thought: Farewell, remembered things!
These are the nights for nerveless sleeping.
Not music with her bells and strings
Could stir me into passion and weeping.

Such quiet ruin is in my breast,
Such peace upon my body has stolen,
I shall have drowned in dreamless rest
Love's memory ere the leaves are fallen.

Wherefore I came into the wood,
For there they fell past knowing or number,
And flung myself in solitude
Among their mindlessness to slumber.

But sleep for once was not my friend
By whom all creatures are befriended.
I wakened in the autumn wind
Hot with the dream that has not ended.

WHAT ARTIFICE

WHAT ARTIFICE against foul time
So difficult, I often cry,
As this I make of air and rhyme?
Oh, any other! I reply.
Yes, any house on any site
Sacred to eagles or to doves,
If a man builds it in delight
And terror, for the one he loves.

The thing his passionate hands devise
His mind reviews with cold despair:
Likely as not a storm will rise
And hurl it down, for all his care;
Likely as not when he has done
And pulled away the props and ropes
His dear will wed another one.
He knows. But while he builds he hopes.

Warm youth with only time to fear
That brings you potions for your pain,
If you come here, and tarry here,
I shall as good as live again.
May you find here, desirous youth,
That wild and deathless fugitive
Whom I have followed—for in truth,
Living with her I long to live.

You waders through the weeds and flowers,
Come rest within my house of words—
And you who toil at loftier towers
Round which the planets play like birds,
And you who fell upon your knees
And heard the roofs of fortune fall.
A house of song will stand for these,
I daresay, if it stands at all.

If it should tumble, let it go.
Give back the ground to wordless things.
When wondering children want to know
What ruin is this beset by wings,
Tell them no matter: something made
In haste and ignorance—as it were
A house where Beauty never stayed.
But tell them it was made for her.

TWO

ANATOMY OF DEATH

I

ONE BEAUTY still is faultless, not
Deflowered in the bed of thought:
It is a sound of sunken seas.
It is an avid wish for ease.
It is the earth, it is the sky
When passion is a lute put by
And life a dancer out of breath.
It is the lovely face of death,
Adored and guessed at—never once
Beheld in chrysoprase or bronze;
Not in the temple or the grove,
Not in a hundred nights of love.

This was the morning sun, the wild
Daybreak of anguish in the child.
This is the sun at noon no less,
Deep in the dome of nothingness.
Wherefore, impoverished heart, be proud
To wear the purple of the shroud.
If you are friendless, take for friend
The noble wave, the affluent wind.
If you are homeless, do not care:
Inhabit the bright house of air.
If you are worn with wayfaring,
Lie down within the arms of spring.

Mind without substance, bright and shadowy,
Blowing above the body, as high, as strong,
As delicate from the flesh sprung
As from the earth a tree,
See
How the sick animal, partaker of your shade too long,
Sleeps without tossing, is construed to dust—
And how the ghost,
Briefly from its outlandish precincts lured,
Thereto returns and leaves you traceless, a bird
Less feathers than song.

Now with no use but to grow big and blacken the noon,
Make phantoms of familiars, come between
The luminous night and love, that is never seen
But by the light of the moon;
Now with no will but the dæmon that has undone you,
The wish that is in your rustling and sighing aloud
To be translated, to be lost and spent
Into a subtler element,
Into tempest or cloud;

Now with the sweet and sap of summer upon you
In the first frosty days
Before the green goes garish and the fall
Puts out your late flamboyance from the bough:
Now,

Ready to hurl yourself a hundred ways
In any wind at all,

Relent, give over, let your limbs be shaken,
Let the wide tyranny of your leaves be shattered—
Into the light and dusk and darkness scattered,
Into the ignorance of the air taken.

III

CRUEL AND lovely, being feared,
Iron, and phosphorus, and air—
Creature of chaos, I have heard—
The body were too much to bear.

Yet be the spirit a little brave,
It were as light as plume on wing,
As light, as brief, as foam on wave,
Or on the world the freight of spring.

Then time would cut the ghostly tether,
And the bright captive blow away
In autumn with the eagle's feather,
The falling leaf, the flying spray.

IV

I AM a dreamer in a dream
Of one who sleeps, as it would seem,
Crowding the darkness with queer shapes,
Like selves imagined: None escapes
From that still body, though it go
Back to the night he cannot know
And twitch along his nerves and start
A senseless sorrow in his heart,
Or quiet him and make him smile;
None but is focused for a while
On his mind's eye ere it withdraws;
No counterfeit of what he was,
Or is, or hopes or dreads to be—
This cinema of you and me
And our rude acts and subtle schemes
And woebegone and sanguine dreams—
Nothing of all things, ill or good,
But plays upon his pulsing blood,
As if to lure him, breath by breath,
That way for life, that way for death.

Whatever dream I call my own—
The body hung upon the bone,
The moods of it that mill the sphere,
The echoed faces far and near,
The sullen eyes, the eyes that shine,
The careless mouths I catch to mine;

All these, and earth, air, water, fire,
The affluence of its desire
Mysterious and manifest;
The sun, that rockets to the west
And vanishes and leaves a white
Shower of suns against the night;
The April morning, half afloat
In flying mist; the rainbow caught
A moment among distant rain;
The leveled grass where I have lain
Here in the shadow of a hill—
That dream is the one dreamer's still.
For faith and science fly to this:
His dreams are mine, and mine are his;
My dreams—since in a world designed
Of sheer, imponderable mind,
The atom stands for all outdoors—
Are infinite, and so are yours.
And death was but a dream I knew,
As only the warm living do
Who dream the direst dreams are true.

All honour be to those who give
Their lives in learning how to live—
Who wear like kings, because they must,
The gypsy-coloured cloak of dust,
Making it fair as may befit
The majesty reduced to it:
Ermined with virtue, sleek and snowy,

Gemmed with the shining eyes of joy.
But some are naked, or they have
No habit but the heavy grave.
They walk unbowed, but bear defeat
Intrinsic in their bodies' weight.
They do not bleed, but entertain
Disaster in the circling vein.
They love and kiss, but they are born
To love the lion or unicorn—
All things impossible and perverse.
They are the spirit's amateurs
On whom time's clothing sits awry
And frets like fetters. Such was I:
Wherefore I studied how to die,

Wherefore I took my way alone,
Citizen of oblivion,
Bedfellow of bird and beast,
Of death the true anatomist;
And that no less for having held
The spirit's essence undispelled.
Here is the beauty only they
Embrace who shudder from the day
Through wretched times and harsh events.
Till the world slays them or relents,
They loathe its interests—they prefer
Eternity for taskmaster.

I was not always one to keep
So payless an apprenticeship.

The moment and the moment's mood
Employed me once. I had for food
The dusty fare of all who die.
Seeing the spirit so put by,
The flesh so polished and impearled,
I thought: It is perhaps a world
As sweet as any, sweet enough
To loiter with and weary of,
Though empty as an ocean shell
Where the lost sighs of wonder dwell.
At length came shouting through myself
Havoc, that broke my heart in half:
Thus did the spirit blunder loose
From its five-bolted charnel house,
To harry ether, in effect,
Not flown, but flying derelict—
And starved in spite, or swooped to share
The wasp's honey of black despair,
While all about were glittering free
The gorgeous pueblos of the bee.

How calm upon the fated sphere
Was I, who hoped for nothing here!
I took misfortune in my teeth,
And found no man to quarrel with.
I mused: The mischief was entire
When earth forsook its parent fire
To spin erroneous in space,
An ember from an idle blaze

Wherein some chemistry awoke
This sick vibration of the rock,
This soreness of the sundered bit,
This life! I longed to fasten it
With all its troubled faiths untried
For ever into the sun's hot side;
But since I could not, learned instead
A few devices of the dead—
Buried my dreams, as it might be,
In barter for a budding tree;
Interred them at the season's fall
On meadows of the mystical
That prosper most in earth's eclipse,
Saying: Here cold enchantment sleeps,
Here love, henceforward a fine wraith,
And murdered out of mercy, faith—
Saying: Let others walk the loud
And endless labyrinth of the crowd,
Detecting in the time-begot
Some dignity they know not what
To fashion out of clay or write
In characters of black and white;
But as for me, I have declared
To hunt a quarry unseen, unheard—
To tell in words a wordless peace
Like the unbreathing lips of Greece,
To paint in pigments of no dye
Such images as may go by
Before her blind, enamelled eye.

I rendered to this aim the whole
Invisible sinew of my soul,
So it would seize me and exert
Its airiness in every part,
Casting for carnal anchorage
Only my hand upon the page—
Which lay there still and did not move,
Unapt to leave a mark but *love*.
Then from the solid home of breath,
The world of dust that wished me death,
The granite ranges risen in greed,
I retched and panted to be freed.
And it may be I died indeed.

Yet April comes, and here am I,
Not knowing if I live or die
And caring less, but caring so
For all clear things that careless grow
I cannot see the buds gone thick
About a tangle of dry stick,
The green swords cutting the black ground,
The robins hearkening around,
But I go loose from head to feet
And lunge along the morning street,
And hang, and lunge—if man or ghost—
From post to wall and wall to post,
Caught in a storm of ecstasy
That lets the gold forsythias be,
A dream of fountains stopped in air,
But drives me to the earth somewhere

Out of the way of all who pass,
And rubs and rolls me in the grass
Down to the bottom of a hill,
And beats on me as if to kill,
Yet leaves me lying and laughing still.

I am among you, ghost or man,
To learn what carelessness I can
Through pain and pleasure, hope and rue.
Death was a double dream I knew,
A savage burial, or brave.
I have returned from either grave.
I have groped onward; I have come
Into a new delirium.
Dying was but the wish for it,
A gross disease or exquisite,
The spirit's or the body's care.
I have patched up the childish pair,
Submitting such divorce is bad:
Without its darling, one goes mad
And takes an incubus to keep—
But that dissolves in brighter sleep
When the warm truant brazens on.
The dreaming of dreams is never done;
I daresay even underground
A man encounters nothing sound.

May you who drift from fraud to fraud
Like phantoms of a sleeping god

Rejoice to tenant, while you may,
A dream that fills the night and day
And furnishes the starlit earth:
There is a kingdom something worth,
Though it were wrought of less than air.
May you be lovely tyrants there
Till all swims round you and is lost—
Wearing with pride, because you must,
The raggle-taggle, ruined dust.

I know what you are thinking of:
That fools do well to laugh and love,
With darkness squeezing for their place
And they as lightly spun as lace.
Go laughing, though. Go loving, though.
Go hounding beauty always. Oh,
Endure the dazzling dream unblurred:
Life, that is reasonless, absurd,
Cruel, unhinging, crazy, sweet,
Incorrigible—life complete,
Not split into a heaven and hell.
However you dream you will but tell
The one who dreams you what to do.
He has no counsellors but you
To keep his heart from hate and gall—
He has no consciousness at all
But in yourselves. As it would seem,
He is a dreamer in a dream.

V

Weep, Aphrodite, for Adonis dead,
As by the gale flung down, a white-gold thing—
His flesh the bloom of orchards early shed,
His shining curls the little leaves of spring.
Weep not for us who perish old and worn,
 Pretenders to your earthly kingdom still
From which you turned the feathered team forsworn;
We come to woe because we do your will.
We come to penury, to paupers' terms—
Usurped by time and taxed of all our breath,
Made host to brigands, even the eyeless worms
That blunder on the dazzling spoils of death:
We come to dust. Yet while that dust endures
The earth is young, and amorous, and yours.

INDEED, WHEN it is done, incredible youth told over,
The times sweet and shameful, the issues shocking and
    sweet,
And his life lying calm like a litter of leaves at his feet,
A man would be nothing but that he has been a lover.
He is glad for that. As for the rest, it is dead.
As for the rest, it is a tedious madness his mind must repeat.
He is one who wakes from a delirium and is told what he
    said.

So disabused, he would surely abandon then
The world and its abject ways, its joyless fever,
Its hatred, its false smiles, its foul conniving—
Yet loves it still, remembering amid all these,
Superb and insolent, the lovers striving:
Amid the frightened world, in thrall for ever
To knaves and clowns and peevish impotent men,
The lovers, free and wanton, wildly at peace;
Remembering still amid its woes and wrongs
The lovers locking tongues.

Here on a spoiling planet everywhere
Life starts from its tireless cisterns, strange, renewed,
In lovers' bodies. It is by no means subdued.
It seethes from its coldness, a quarrel of ice in the sun,
And the old fears go under, every one—
The frigid thoughts, the freezing in harsh weather
Of that bright torrent into immobile shapes:

It shudders from each paralysis, escapes
Each cold design a season caught together.

Here also in lovers' bodies, let it be granted,
The spirit sojourns and is by no means undone:
Here, being snared with time's most cunning snare
Of conscious dust and its venereal engines,
The spirit grows most brave, forgets to care,
Lies laughing at the enemy, by no means daunted,
Takes up those toils and wears them with a vengeance,
Bone, flesh, and muscle—finds them light as air.
Thus even these are a moment wholly aware,
A moment before they weary are wholly enchanted,
The ghost being actual in the earthen mesh—
The mystery, flesh:

Thus on the planet incessantly everywhere
The blood remembers its freedom, rises afresh,
Destroys the cold austerities that shackle.
Here is the very noise of spring, debacle
As of proud waters not to be stayed by winter.

There is no kingdom lovers may not enter,
Making of themselves a marvellous beast with two heads:
There is no mythic land where time goes by
Forgotten—land intenser to the eye
Than that of the living, land lonelier than the dead's—
Lovers may not inhabit. And if any cry
Can sound beyond a world so lost in the sky,
It is the crying of lovers in their beds.

Indeed, a man is rejoiced to live and die,
Remembering love—how, even long ago
And ignorantly, and with but little faith,
He too looked out a moment past life and death.

Here was no easy wedding, in a wink,
Of dust with dust, to be at odds no more;
Here was no mere nostalgia to throw
The weight of the mind to earth, and not to think—
For when desire had fathomed to the core
The frenzied dust, and laid the body low,
It flew insatiate from the body's brink
With a more sovereign need than dust could know.

Here was no idle fetch for breeding woe
To a woeful house, or pride to a proud estate—
Not merely tenderness, though that is much,
Nor the loins' luxury, though that is great.
Say rather, here was such longing as would have known
A million times more beauty than the body could touch.

Here, for a moment, a man got free from fear
And struggled against doom in the flesh and bone;
Another moment, and he might have got
Free from the fatal mechanism of his thought:
So would its wheels go silent upon the wall
And in the universe for ever. Here,
By leave of any light-hearted encounter at all,
The body hoped, and heard the spirit's call,

And would have followed—would have ventured forth
From time's vile ruins beyond the temporal
And known the unknowable loveliness naked and near;
Would have surprised the seasons of the year
And slaked itself upon the turning earth,
Would have possessed the sun, the stars, the moon—
But fell asleep too soon.

VII

EARTH, YOU have never torn apart
A poppy, or a pink undone,
But you have woven another one,
Nearer the image in your heart.

Summer has wearied and gone sear,
And yet your hands beneath the hill
Were busy with her blossoms still,
Making them fairer year by year.

Accept this darling of the dust,
This being where your summers blend.
Truly, he travels in the end
To you—and he is yours, I trust.

Should he go down with none to heed
And perish unaccounted for,
It would be autumn evermore,
It would be wintertime indeed.

Doomed promiser of deathless spring,
Behold the strangeness of a man.
If you destroy him, do you plan
To fashion a more marvellous thing?

Knowing as little as I know,
Feeling a knowledge more than mine
In the mute trance of tree and vine,
I am persuaded it is so.

I am content. Take back your own:
Take back the golden leaves that fall,
The roses from the garden wall—
Take back the body from the bone.

Drink up its lovely dreams like dew,
And let the spiders spin among
That trellis where all sweetness hung,
And let the rain drip through.

THREE

WHO TRACK THE TRUTH

QUICK AND intangible as ever the quarry,
Now thought no more a phœnix of the air—
But now what murderous padding sublunary
Lithe thing, let them who track the truth declare.

They have come home, to die of eating and drinking.
They say it is useless, tracking hour by hour
What twists away into the wilds past thinking,
Or only turns to deafen and devour.

Yet these are they who in the night stole near it
When it would pause, and pant, and put behind
An instant its green eyes of desolate spirit,
Like jewels in the darkness of a mountain unmined.

And young men still, because indeed they are younger,
Lay down their girls and glasses—hoping at least
For a hero's life, or a death from thirst and hunger,
Or a bright look of the beast.

SEPTEMBER MOON

ABOVE THE continent I saw appear
For the last time in the last warmth of the year
The gibbous moon. I thought: It comes to shed
A last kind beam to kiss and loiter by
On all things derelict or left to die,
Being itself a thing abandoned and dead.
Now let all creatures hounded out of doors,
Love's waifs and felons whom the world abhors,
Make holiday until the cold rains start.
This moon goes with them, even as my heart.

And when it laid my shadow at my feet
I thought of all things infamous and sweet,
All wayward craft whereon the moon is bright:
Of poor consanguines helplessly possessed
In the tall glittering cornfields of the west—
Of girl and girl in the New England night
For whom dead Lesbos lives—of boy and boy
Somehow surviving Crete in Illinois—
Of ladies and their lovers mouth to mouth
Deep in the south.

AUTUMN MOVEMENT

Friends I have had, the dæmon-driven, the gay,
The girls like blossoms, the games and dancing done,
(Voices half-heard, and laughter far away)
You are my loneliness when night comes on,

And I am alone. You are the rumour in my blood
Of footsteps flying on every guessed-at trail.
You are a story scarcely understood
That I must strive to tell for ever, and fail.

For there is no way I should want it told, in the end,
But in the old alphabets of earth, to be
Extant as the leaves' literature on the wind
When wind and earth have had their way with me.

Time has its poems, though it writes them slower.
The rock remembers—it has worked its art.
The dust forgets. O footsteps going nowhere,
How brief your hieroglyphs upon my heart!

This is my loneliness, in the idle hours
When autumn and night lean in, and I am alone,
Remembering friends I have had, the girls like flowers,
Remembering the games and dancing done.

EXTEMPORARY LINES

In Celebration of a Treaty

LET EVERY promise be broken,
But not this one.
Let lovers give back their pledges and have done;
Let spring's intelligence be spoken
And hushed in a fabulous autumn without end;
And let a friend be faithless to a friend.

But this were too much treason:
That man deliver himself into the prison
Of his own mind, and turn the rusty key,
Having once from those archaic walls won free.
This cannot be:
That he forego all honour and betray
The truce he makes with his own heart today;
Or that his lips recant, which utter now
One lucid vow
Into the face of ruin and unreason.

Here is a task that will not let him sleep;
A tool more difficult to wield by far
Than the bright instruments of war:
This peace his hands must keep
Against the malcontent that rankles deep
In vassals, and the avarice of lords.
Here is a trust more solemn than a sword's.

And if he fail in this; if the vision dim;
If he go vagrant from the valorous plan;
If he endure an old unslaken
Animal within the blood to waken—
Let him be always something less than man:
Let time, that long ago untaloned him,
Restore the beast in visage and in limb;
Let him be horned and hairy,
Stupid and wary,
Running astonished from the ocean's rim.

And let his little world become his tomb,
Sink from the starlight into something less:
It never sprung to flame but for his courage
Or wove one flower but of his consciousness.
Let it grow bare, forget to burn and bloom,
Deny its fallen despot warmth or forage,
Flash out no more in ether—hide its face
Like a spent swimmer in the surf of space.

FANTASIA OF WINTER

Impalpable python, go wrap the world in your rings,
Till the earth's ragged floor is pressed to a pane of glass
Imprisoning petals and cobwebs and grackles' wings
And the brown ghosts of grass.

Go—delicate, relentless, without sound,
Insatiate, swift—seize beauty as a bird is seized:
So let the promise be kept, the sick profound
Anticipation appeased.

For here in the hollow of my grief you have been harboured
    and fed,
Privily from the world in its season of butterflies.
Here, hollowed out with bitterness, I have given you bed,
Winter, serpent of ice!

Secret, intolerable, here you have lain the summer's length:
It is enough. Stir! Waken! Uncoil! Wind
Across the world your cold translucent strength,
Terrible sleeper within the mind.

ELEGY

I SHALL LOSE your face in the riot of strange faces
That rush toward mine all day.
At night I shall go to the nervous, crowded places.
I shall concentrate on the people and the play,
And follow along to the dancing, and be gay.

I shall lose your voice in the anarchy of voices,
The rustle of wheels and footsteps and the wind.
I shall listen all day, I shall learn innumerable noises
To disentangle from what the city has dinned—
And at the end,
Waiting for sleep, I shall think of music, or say
Old rhymes, or pray.
All this to frighten the ghost of one sound away.

All this to frighten away one ghost who would start
Perilously into my blood by day and by night,
Perilously upon my mouth with the remembered kiss
Like a paralysis,
Till I am wound in your beauty as in a tightened net,
And suddenly it is enough, and I must forget.

I know the way. I shall lose part by part,
So all is lost but the insensible thing—
The dream, the image not of sound or sight:
It is a wild perfume upon the world, it is the bright
Perpetual honey in the hive of spring,
It is the broken bell whose legends ring
Fatally and for ever in my heart.

SOLILOQUY ALONG A SIDEWALK

THE CHOOSERS between glad and sorrowful love
Are not for me. I must let them come to their choice.
I must love them with the corner of my eye; I must keep
My hands in my pockets, or I shall touch and betray them.
I took them in play. But when they teased me for promises
I could only laugh, or get choked and blinded. I,
Knowing myself, acknowledging my mystery,
Being nothing single but all things in confusion,
Prepared like soil for the flowering of the mind—
I, capable of everything but denial,
Must banish myself from these. Theirs are the bodies
That make my dreams too sweet to wake from. Theirs
The doorways where I turn to ice and flame,
Fish for a cigarette, and am gone.

WOMAN WITHOUT FEAR

How BEAUTIFUL is a woman whose avarice is over.
She is content that time should take what it will.
She is proud to have no pride. She asks of her lover
Love only, for good or ill.

She makes of her body a strange bed till morning
Wherein he breathes oblivion better than sleep;
And when he wakes she is nowhere—she has fled without
    warning,
And left him nothing to keep

But the trace of her tears on the pillow, and a bright strand
Out of her hair, and happiness, and a little grief
That is but the weight of a plum-petal in the hand,
Or heart-shaped mulberry leaf.

THE DEAD ELM ON THE HILLTOP

THIS TREE was burned by lightning to its root
In an October tempest many years ago now.
I can remember the lovely range of its bough,
Its scattered fruit,

Its voice as of waters on an invisible shore,
And the veined leaves transparent against the sky:
And so I have thought this tree could not die till I die.
Yet April comes no more

In a tall cloud of bronze to the top of the hill,
And summer stands no more in singing green,
And autumn, returning like a murderer to the scene,
Finds nothing left to kill.

MEMORY OF LAKE SUPERIOR

I KNOW a country of bright anonymous beaches
Where the sand sleeps unprinted till it is stone.
Granite grows loud among the hills and ditches
Of the blown water when the water is blown.

Up on the mountain the sky is everywhere,
The lake fallen hugely underfoot as if
Into the bottom of a well of air,
The island upon it little as a leaf.

The woods are dark with the rank lace of hemlock and pine,
Beech, birch, and balsam, and the shadow of these.
There are mushrooms, and thimbleberries sweeter than
    wine,
And a far noise of wind in the tops of the trees.

That country was all the knowledge I shall ever learn;
It was all the wisdom I shall ever have.
It was there I looked for the driftwood boughs that burn
In colours like a memory of the wave.

It was there I looked along the forest floor
For the grey feather of the grouse's wing.
It was there I learned to look for nothing more,
Looking into the sea-blue eyes of spring.

THE CONSTANT ONE

WHEN LOVE was false and I was full of care,
And friendship cold and I was sick with fear,
Music, the beautiful disturber of the air,
Drew near,

Saying: Come with me into my country of air
Out of the querulous and uncivil clay;
Fling down its aching members into a chair,
And come away,

And enter the wide kingdom beyond despair
Where beauty dwells unaltering, even such
As my invisible body made of air
Time cannot touch.

Take back your dreams, or take oblivion there,
Or an old madness setting memories free—
Or if all else has vanished into air,
Take me.

FOUR

ADDRESS TO THE DOOMED

I

SAY IT is life that matters. Say the bone
And flesh that blazoned it are but a book
Mislaid, forgotten, and the meaning known.
I will believe, but I have lived to look
On the cold body of the beautiful dead,
White and immobile as the moon in air—
The imperious heart being strangely quieted,
And the proud spirit flown I know not where.
Say it is earth again. Let it be hid
In ruined leaves. Account it as the dust
That quarrels not with doom and never did,
And reckon me among the quick who must.
Yet would I sleep tonight at the rose's root,
Seeing what Time has trampled underfoot.

II

BELIEVE ME, then, because my mood is black,
And hear me out, because my words are few:
I have not gazed on autumn to give back
The garlands of the withering Grove to you,
Or learned upon the ruined Porch to say
So be it to the passing of a leaf
That falls forgotten on a frosty day;
I come to you as one apprised of grief.
Yet courage more than wisdom—or as much
As will avail when words are nothing worth,
Lest you be old too soon at sorrow's touch
And fling yourself untimely on the earth—
I can bequeath you, as the dead bequeath
Life to the dust that it may live and breathe.

III

I SEE how the forgetful earth replies,
Though plundered yearly, to the year's warm humour,
And leads new life, to stand with innocent eyes,
Unwarned, unweaned, upon the sill of summer.
I see her trust and her betrayal clearly—
The beaks of shivering birds put up to beg,
The hawthorn bloom upon the branch too early,
The snake unwinding from the stolen egg.
Yet since the heart's dismay were but a shadow
Weightless on earth as of a flying wing,
Or autumn leaf upon a flowering meadow
Caught in the quick machinery of spring—
Let the doomed brave be born and slapped to breath:
I take these tidings to my master Death.

IV

FEAR NOT to die, though you must feel the cold
Shadow of all things that the sun has shown:
The body with its bright excess of gold
Blowing to silver ere the sun goes down;
The earth and the wild issue of her womb—
The ape that drags its knuckles from afar,
The pulsing fish, the bird on rigid plume.
You bear their blindness, being what you are.
Being the weariest creature and the last,
The sigh of God upon the seventh day,
You keep the bestial chrysalis uncast
And the wing folded that would fly away.
What do you fear of dying? That will be
To drop the world like fetters and go free.

V

FEAR NOT to live, for life is proud and long
Past the grave's ignominy to undo.
As men peered outward when the earth was young
Dreaming of shores unsailed for, so may you.
So of the timeless mystery may you take
Your amorous will—though nevermore from Spain
The little ships with laughter in their wake
Will sail to the Americas again.
This is your home, the hemisphere they won:
It is a lovely land—so high, so wide,
You may ascend its mountains to the sun
And step into the sea on either side.
Yet even now, in the enamoured mind,
This were another port to put behind.

VI

WHAT THOUGH your fathers be accounted slaves?
What though the dunce in every schoolroom know
They fought and killed at the caprice of knaves?
Surely your fathers' fathers were not so.
Obedient they but to a dream, who went—
Dumb, driven, by Beauty none the less beguiled—
Out of an island over a continent,
Like a slow thought through the unthinking wild.
Yours be their hunger, not the food they found;
Yours be the pathlessness beyond the west;
Yours be the dream unravished—not the round
Planet explored, disputed, and possessed,
The map emblazoned and the boundaries drawn.
Earth is behind you: Let the mind march on.

VII

Would you be warranted some reward as well?
Look at the heaven of which the psalmists sing;
Look at the world the advertisements tell—
And turn away, and seek the beautiful thing.
And be persuaded, Beauty cannot die
While there are minds to know her, who is not
Established only in the startled eye
But in the calm acropolis of thought.
To her alone this refuge shall be pledged:
Then may the naughty will of Time be done—
Then may the body, like a town besieged,
Tremble and fall for ever from the bone—
Yet she shall suffer not the sacking hand.
The city falls. The citadel will stand.

VIII

I SAW the globe that sails the starry dark
As never galleon into nothingness
Was launched before—as never Noah's ark
With such dear lading in such long distress;
And none to captain her upon that sea
Or hold a compass when the heavens are blind,
And no intelligence of what's to be,
Even from the highest crow's nest of the mind.
I thought: May we who voyage here be brave
As never seafarers were brave before,
So be this vessel worthy of the wave
She will come proud to the appointed shore.
Or is the ship already scuttled? Then
Let the rats scurry—let the men be men.

IX

THE EARTH is honoured, for she keeps your history—
Her paths are lovely, for they show your way;
Her tombs are fragrant, for they tell your mystery,
Ambiguous tenant of the simple clay.
Metal and adamant, the heavens wheeling
Above the wayward ball look down unmoved—
Yet here the rock is disarrayed, revealing
What Time has murdered and what men have loved.
As a lost hunter in the howling north
Who borrows refuge where a camp has been—
The bed of pine-boughs and the smouldering hearth—
So have you found one planet warm and green:
A home till spring, a hearth to build a fire on,
Against that blizzard blowing stone and iron.

X

REMEMBER, though the telescope extend
Few manifestoes Time may not efface
When earth has wandered to her freezing end
And left no footprint on the paths of space,
How of all living creatures you alone
Surmise exclusion from the secret plan—
You, with the cipher cut into your own
Most unimaginable substance, Man.
Afraid! Afraid! Yet the bright skies you fear
Were black as doom, were but the want of skies,
Were nothing at all until you happened here,
Bearing the little lanterns of your eyes.
In the first gathering of the ultimate frost
Remember this, and let the world be lost.

Afternoon

I came to an orchard - blossoms blowing
On twisted branches, trees inclined
By wind, all lunging west and throwing
Their shadows parallel behind.

A frail green wave of rain swept in
Flashing the sun like broken glass.
It threaded slanting through the thin
Black boughs; I stayed to see it pass.

It hurried out across the meadows
And in a wide bright mist was gone.
I stayed to watch the orchard shadows—
Crawl east an inch, then wandered on;
But very soon I heard a mutter
Along the dusty road afresh,
And when I reached the pond the water
Was silver rings in a windy mesh.

                                   "Boy in the Wind"